Modern Artists   Chillida

Harry N. Abrams, Inc., Publishers, New York

Pierre Volboudt

Chillida

Translated from the German by Vivienne Menkès

Library of Congress Catalog Card Number: 67-30344

Heraclitus's maxim that conflict is the father of all things applies to sculpture more than to any other branch of the arts. The sculptor is in conflict with space, which he usurps and appropriates to his own ends, and with matter, from which the nascent form must struggle free. Space, the more abstract of the two elements, must submit to the imposition of concrete form. The more recalcitrant material, on the other hand, is better suited to participate actively in the struggle which is the essence of the sculptor's work, and which wrings movement from the inert mass, gives substance to the immaterial, enriches solid matter with fantasy, and makes visible the secret essence of forms. The inner spirit that is form consists in the living resolution of antitheses into a rich and complex synthesis.

Chillida's work clearly illustrates this conflict. We are faced with it anew in each powerful line. It was the artist who threw down the gauntlet, and in so doing he took upon himself the consequences, the discord which spurs him on. This decision has determined the form of his work and the direction of his thought ever since he became a sculptor. As he pursues his goal, which lies at the end of a path full of long yet inevitable detours, the decisions he has made are translated into tangible shapes; his thoughts return continually to their starting-point, contradict each other and close in gradually on the object of their quest.

Two factors converge in Chillida: an inflexible and undeviating inspiration, and the mysterious legacy of collective imagination which has for generations retreated into its own untamed inner fastnesses. The dangerous tension between the two forms of existence in which the Spanish consciousness comes to terms with its own plenitude and its own contradictions, *ser y estar*, combines with a stern fatalism to produce a mysterious, ascetic tradition entrenched behind its own defences. The abrupt and unforthcoming Spanish sensibility withdraws into a savage realm of sombre and unending dreams, where man is bound to nature by a pact of which the different clauses have never been announced. Chillida is a Basque, and acknowledges his kinship to the spiritual race of those Spaniards who have transmuted a parched and arid reality into subdued passion, glowing strength and lucid delirium. Aware of the contradictions within him, Chillida lays claim to his heritage.

He was born on 10 January 1924 in San Sebastián, and apart from frequent visits abroad, mainly to France, where he spent several years, he has lived and worked in his home town ever since. San Sebastián is the capital of the province of Guipúzcoa, one of the seven provinces which make up the Basque country and one of the three, known as the Irurac Bat, which have belonged to Castile since the Middle Ages. The individuality of the Basque country, divided today between France and Spain, is found in its purest form in this region. Chillida's spiritual heritage is that of a Basque.

But what does being a Basque involve? Principally it means owing allegiance to a community which jealously preserves the features distinguishing it from other communities. Its origins are legendary or even mythological. The Basque adheres fiercely to his convictions; he feels bound by immemorial traditions. His character, tough and harsh and uninterested in literary fictions, offers him a form of defence, as do the endless difficulties of his ancient language. He is very close to nature, in which he worships occult forces and the power of the elements. He has a special feeling for metal, allegedly introduced into the southern valleys of the Pyrenees by the first blacksmith, Tubal Cain, son of Lameth, 3000 years before our era; a dance called *Ezpata-Dantza* is performed in its honour. He worships water flowing in the narrow mountain ravines, and the south wind, *Haice-Hegoa*, which dominates the whole land. When the south wind blows, ancient passions are kindled and men remember the days of witchcraft.

Perhaps Chillida's work owes something to these atavistic instincts. His sculptures have a very close affinity with their material and acquire from it not only their plastic qualities, but also their symbolic and elemental character. Iron takes on the form of the unknown, becomes the tuning-fork of unseen vibrations and the "comb of the winds"; wood is transformed into a framework of tightly contained forces. Chillida dignifies the crafts of the blacksmith and the carpenter and borrows their traditional techniques—soldering, dove-tailing and mortising.

If we want to see how the forms take shape, there is no need to visit the sculptor's studio, for each carries within it the secret of its own development. Only the artist's eye can visualize the ultimate form to be taken by the piece of iron awaiting its destiny in his workshop and the pieces of wood hanging from the pulleys. He alone can detect the hidden flaw which cries out for final correction, for he alone can recognize perfection.

So we must turn to the artist. We learn more from listening to the movement of his thoughts than from watching the concentrated energy of his body as he works. The silent dialogue between man and work is interrupted every now and then by a brief comment, explanation or anecdote. Chillida tells how one day he saw a beam lying beside his path, bought it on the spot and carried it off, without any idea what he was going to do with it. He quotes St John of the Cross and his inspired visions. When talking about his sculptures, which are frequently rectangular, he mentions Herreras, the architect of the Escurial and allegedly the author of a treatise on the cube. He describes an incident, quotes a reminiscence, mentions some experience.

He speaks hesitantly, carefully considering the problems raised by the questions one puts to him, and talking with a kind of stubborn passion which seems to be struggling against some inner resistance; his gaze is fixed on the inner reality of which he is attempting to describe the contours and disclose the workings.

"A cloud of birds in the sky is better than a single one in the hand." This saying appears on the wall of his studio. For Chillida it is a motto, a challenge to achieve the impossible, and he lets it guide his thoughts and his way of life. If an artist always aims towards something which lies beyond the form, risks what is certain for the sake of something which appears to be unattainable, then he is voluntarily calling into question the very concept which underlies his work.

"In the work which you see here in the studio or in a few museums or galleries I have occasionally managed to ensnare one of these 'clouds of birds'. Others have slipped through my fingers. When I'm sure of one of them and have it firmly in my grasp, my thoughts have already turned to the next one and to all the others which I dream about. I never know which of the clouds I shall manage to capture. Gradually it begins to take shape—at first I can scarcely make it out, then it becomes clearer and then sometimes vanishes again. But when I've once captured the idea I never let it go. All I have to do is to leave it to develop."

"A piece of iron is an idea in itself, a powerful and unyielding object. I must gain complete mastery over it, and force it to take on the tension which I feel within myself, evolving a theme from dynamism. Sometimes the iron refuses to give in. But when I eventually reach my goal I always know; the individual fragments crystallize with a sudden shock and form a whole. Nothing can now separate the space from the form which encircles it."

"Sculpture is a function of space. I am not concerned with the space which lies outside the form, which surrounds the volume and in which the shapes dwell, but with the space actually created by the shapes, which dwells in them and is all the more effective when it works in secret. I might perhaps compare it to the life-giving breath which causes the form to swell up and contract and makes visible that inner psychic space which is hidden from the outside world. To me this space is not something abstract, but forms a reality as concrete as the reality of the volumes which enclose it. It must be as tangible as the form in which it is revealed, for it has a character of its own. It sets in motion the matter which encloses it; it determines its proportions and scans and regulates its rhythms. It must find a corresponding echo in us and it must possess a kind of spiritual dimension. In the same way, any room I live in, for however brief a period, must harmonize with an ideal pattern which corresponds to my actions and which also governs them. Some rooms are suffocating—one is stifled by them, one feels physically unwell; this type of room is uninhabitable. The same is true of sculpture. I am always searching for a space which conforms with the dynamic image of which I spoke earlier. Volumes exist only in relation to this unseen element; the essence of a sculpture must make its presence felt and transpose its inner harmony to the world of externals."

"That is also why I never make rough models. I never work on anything but the actual sculpture. The work is its own model and corrects itself as I work on it. The rhythm becomes more precise, swells and changes until it eventually finds the right tempo. This type of spatial figure cannot be fully defined in advance. Anyone trying to do so would be putting the finishing touches to a work of art before it had even been started. At first it is no more than a vague, almost indefinable suggestion, a sensation which has yet to take shape. And this shape grows with every correction and with every fresh attack on it. Drawing is no way of approaching a sculpture. At first I used to do a good deal of drawing, both left-handed and right-handed. It was simple, far too simple. Drawing entails laying down boundaries and chaining down the space as it tries to escape. One must think of space in terms of plastic volume, not pin it down on the surface of a flat piece of paper. I can visualize space only in three dimensions. It is three-dimensionality which gives the form its structure; it arises naturally from the requirements of space, which constructs its own outer cover in the way that an animal grows its shell. Like the animal in its shell I am the architect of inner space."

"Form is the product of unceasing and ever-renewed efforts. A single wave means nothing; but one wave follows another and the arrival of each one presupposes the arrival of the next—and of all those to come. Without the steady force of water the single wave would collapse and dissolve. Together they form a single huge entity. No one would think of singling out a note from a symphony. Each note owes its existence to the whole movement of the music; it swells, the individual notes are superimposed one on the other, and then it finally dies away. Sculpture and music exist in the same harmonious and ever developing space. The volume of musical sound fills the silence with tension; similarly there could be no volume in sculpture without the emptiness of space. In the void the form can continue to vibrate beyond its own limits; the space and the volume together, selecting from all the potential structures inherent in the form, build up its final shape. The rhythm is determined by the form and is renewed with it, but lies hidden in the intervals (particularly in the intervals, I should say) between its modulations and variations. I have sometimes tried to express this by means of lines and stresses cut into plaster or lead reliefs. But these relief drawings had no third dimension and so lacked precisely that empty space which is the visible and almost concrete resonance of sculpture."

"A play on surfaces—that's what it really is, frozen music, with no echo. I like sculpture to be clean and clear cut, but it must also be able to extend itself, to twist round and create a feeling of distance; it must be able to create silence or emptiness, whichever you like to call it, so that the form can vibrate. This should perhaps remind us of Basque music, in which the melodies are always changing from major to minor, so that it depends on the listener whether he hears it in one mode or the other. In most of my sculptures positive forms alternate with negative ones. Each is to a certain extent the counterpart and counter-melody of the other. The Basques love music, and their own music is harsh and heavy, like an accompaniment to old and forgotten rites."

"This possible link was confirmed one day when I asked an electrician to come and repair the wiring. It was dark when he came, and in my workshop there were just a couple of candles, which didn't give out much light. When the man had finished he locked round without any sign of surprise. "Yes," he said, "I can understand that. It's like music.""

"But it was only gradually that I managed to make the transition from the solid and impenetrable mass, which allows of no resonance, to the modulation of the form. My first sculpture, executed in 1948, was the torso of a horseman, in plaster and deliberately archaic. It doesn't exist any more. At that time I believed firmly in the importance of volume and thought that everything depended on it. I was preoccupied with solid volumes to which space was external. But something was missing. How could I incorporate this something into these solid forms where everything took place on the surface? I was searching for something different; but I didn't know what it was. I was living in Villènes at the time and saw few people. Yet I wasn't lonely, because I was given very strong support. My father had set out to train my visual memory, my feeling for dimension and proportion, from a very early age, and he would certainly have preferred to see me carry on with my architectural studies, but he accepted the fact that my only interest was in art and also supported me financially. Without him, and without my wife's help and understanding and the sincere and generous friendship of Palazuelo, I might not have persevered. It is mainly thanks to Palazuelo that I managed to overcome the dejection, depression and doubt which dogged me. I knew exactly where I wanted to get to, but I couldn't see how to get there.

Palazuelo was older than I was, and had already made the difficult transition which confronted me. He couldn't show me the way; in the face of the unknown we are always alone. The right path doesn't appear until we have gone astray many times and had many disheartening experiences. Palazuelo led me on when I hesitated and gave me the courage to win through."

"I was working at the time on a relief for the San Sebastián sportsground but I accomplished nothing to satisfy myself. I wanted to go back to the torso and yet at the same time felt that its possibilities were exhausted. I would have to risk a leap in the dark and yet I still shrank from doing so. In spite of this I still didn't want to give up. I returned to Spain and from May to October 1950 settled at Hernani, which is very close to San Sebastián. I suddenly had the idea of making a stele and decided to execute one in iron. Up to now I had never ventured to use this material and so I had to learn a completely new technique. The village black-smith put his workshop at my disposal and I used to take his place in the early mornings before he started work and in the evenings after he'd finished. I learnt how to handle bellows and to stoke the fire. It was a tough apprenticeship."

"This was how I made my first abstract sculpture, which was influenced by the disk-shaped stelae on Basque graves. Their origin is still puzzled over by historians. I called this sculpture *Ilarik* (pl. 4). I decided to use iron in future, for I felt that its relative flexibility would help me to put my vague ideas into practice. Stone is a compact material, and a block of stone is an intractable thing; it repels space. Now what I was really concerned with was using space as my real material; the iron was intended to be merely an expedient, to provide the strings and bow which would help the space to resonate."

"In this I was resuming contact with an age-old inheritance. In the Basque stelae we are struck by the need to treat reality geo-metrically, and this is characteristic of all the earliest Basque monuments. In the Basque provinces we can find geometrically conceived figures of Christ with stiff limbs reminiscent of the spokes of those wheel-like suns round which space seems to revolve."

"You have to be very familiar with metal or wood before they will submit to being tailored to your thoughts. You have to adapt yourself to their character, anticipate their reactions, and demand no more of them than they are capable of giving. You must provoke them with caution. If you follow these rules they will give more than you expect of them; they will radiate inspiration. They are highly receptive. The iron resounds in a sort of musical rhythm, which causes our nerves to vibrate in resonance; it rings beneath the blows of the hammer and the blasts of the bellows; it is as taut as the strings of a musical instrument and it therefore picks up every sound. There is a wild and beautiful Basque word, which rumbles and roars; it is a cry which shepherds sing to each other from miles away, over rocks and mountains, a word which has come down to us from an age filled with the cries of half-wild mountain flocks and the howling of the wind in mountain gorges and the voice of the waves clashing against the reefs of the Cantabrian coast. The word is '*irrintzina*'. Doesn't it make you think of iron ringing on the anvil, or the tough, sharp sound of a tuft of sea grass bending and bristling beneath the whiplash of the wind?"

"This force which I detect in wood and iron is merely the beat and rhythm of something which I feel to be immanent. Although I am the one who determines the outer form, I am simply obeying, in and through the form, that necessity which decrees the development of all living forms. When I begin I have no idea where I'm going. All I can see is a certain spatial constellation from which lines of strength gradually emerge. A direction makes itself felt; and sometimes it leads me where I have never penetrated before, compels me to take first one new direction, and then another—both equally unexpected. I always trust to instinct, the feeling for plastic which I feel within me. At first this feeling is barely perceptible, but as it grows clearer it becomes all the more compelling. I am pursuing a path; I perceive something that I call, for want of a more appropriate word, the 'emanation' of a form; I gradually absorb it and as it were inhale it."

"In art every problem has its own peculiar flavour. When a new development occurs other problems become entangled with it, yet it remains basically the same. It may be taken up afresh, complicated, modified or enriched with variants—that doesn't mean that the basic problem changes. Sometimes it is solved and no more changes are possible. Afterwards it will look different, although it is really the same. It is the same because it appeals to what is essential in us. At the same time it is no longer the same because we have meanwhile advanced a stage further, because we are looking at it differently and approaching it from a different angle, because we have been able to step back from it."

"The artist's attitude to his work is like a spiral. That's why I have so often harked back to a spiral in my sculptures. A spiral is the geometric representation of a movement which only seems to swerve away from its target so that it can encircle in its detours and curves all conceivable possibilities inherent in a spatial figure. In this figure there is an alternation between emptiness and mass, which are bound to a common axis. It reminds me of the way in which a bird of prey circles its hunting-ground. My spiral lies at the heart of the volume, in the vacuum in which the soul of the work crystallizes, the invisible centre of its evolution."

For a natural sculptor the only true material is stone. In stone the living form attains the dignity of the elemental matter from which it has been wrested. Chillida's torso acquires its pent-up energy from the non-form from which it has been released (pl. 1). Meanwhile his stele reaches up to achieve an immediate presence and yet eludes the eye because of its indefinable shapes. It is a symbol in which the abstract and schematic quality of disarticulated form, and the nakedness of immobility lose themselves in a new unity (pl. 4). But iron, too, has its own unique merits. For the artist who prefers iron to any other material its main advantage lies in the fact that it is not passive. The hardest marble can resist the sculptor's chisel only at the expense of its own substance; the only possible "answer" is for the stone to be splintered. Iron, on the other hand, can stand up to such a treatment. It is up to the artist to take a variety of steps to bring the iron to the point where conflict is possible: he must use the precautionary measures, tricks and artifices which in old tracts about the *ars metallica* were connected with a mystic scenario, with a learned yet ingenuous ritual. The smith is the "master of the fire" and makes it his ally and accomplice. Whereas the potter has to entrust his work to the fire for better or worse, the smith collaborates with it. This involves eliminating the element of chance and seizing on the exact moment when the material, having undergone its ordeal by fire, submits and thereby comes to life.

If his design so demands, Chillida polarizes his creative tension in a new medium. He exchanges iron for wood (pls. 36–39). Pieces of wood which have a living structure of their own are fitted into power systems, into a framework which sets like against like. A power of attraction, running in straight lines, links them to an inaccessible centre in which the weight of the masses is concentrated. Horizontal and diagonal movement seems to impart a floating lightness to such pieces.

When seen as a linear element, substance in Chillida's work is at first no more than a thrust forward into space, a rocket which cleaves space asunder. As the form grows, so its pressure increases. The space becomes more solid and more concentrated as the form encloses it with firm thrusts, rigid parallel lines and whiplash curves. It becomes so compressed that the taut, compact forms seem about to envelop it entirely. Yet the form's sole task is to make space visible, either by being surrounded and compressed by it, or by dissecting it and enclosing it so that it becomes the form's hidden core.

The shapes of Chillida's earliest iron sculptures, with their abrupt edges and their sudden curves, form a sort of cage whose hollow centre is furrowed by sharp stakes (pl. 13). There is no superfluous detail to disturb the austere conception underlying them. Chillida subjugates the material to his will. The symbols and rhythms of these pieces are arranged with the precision of a calligrapher. When we look at the black, imperious characters we are inevitably reminded of Cantabrian rock-drawings. The form has been hardened in the furnace, and retains the energy to which it owes its origin. Stiff shafts, unending antennae and sharp hooks are dove-tailed like the links in a chain—a continuity resulting from hidden joints. There is a crystallized harmony in the bunched up lines of force and spatial axes, in the tufts of spears, claws and stings.

The sign is still no more than an ideogram of energy values, an abstract hieroglyph in which space is expressed through volumes. The form results from the co-operation of space and volume, from their cohesion and contrast. It is a spatial form defined by the fixed contours of invisible surfaces, by wide hiatuses, sudden sharp turns and pregnant intervals. Even the boundaries set by the concrete data of form are continually overstepped. In this field of force vibratory modulations are converted into the tangible themes of a "hidden music". In *In Praise of Fire* and *In Praise of Air* (pls. 12, 14), motion is communicated to inertia, the definite is communicated to the vague, the powerfully articulated is communicated to the unformed.

The form is anchored in space with increasing determination. From now on Chillida's sculpture is born of the fission of planes and the splitting up of weighty volumes. Continuity is sharply broken, and the form's development by leaps and jolts can at any moment turn back on itself. The anatomy of these sculptures appears when the rod-shaped bars, hot from the forge, are broken (pls. 17–19). The form is completed in a series of deviations and the orientation is changed from time to time by their subtly calculated angles. To the eyes of the onlooker, these abrupt changes merely provoke movement. But each change of direction upsets the balance and has to be counteracted by the next section. The changes of intensity do not affect the general direction of the sculpture; indeed, if anything, they accentuate it.

The metal, pliable and yet assertive, responds to all these encroachments. In many myths of the Creation the smith-creator gives life to creatures resembling man by breaking their bones. In the same way the hammer separates the individual pieces which make up the work of art. Each blow is a lightly sketched movement. The joints are then notched together. The form shows evidence of a series of irrevocable gestures which diversify and complicate it, in the process of adapting themselves to a system of undeviating asymmetries.

Caesuras make the form supple and yet it is taut to the point of cracking; its current of force continues unabated from one end to the other, but it is constantly held in check. Its course, whether spiral or unswerving, (for one does not exclude the other in Chillida's work), is determined with the help of extraordinarily simple sketches. Chillida's brushstrokes furrow the white paper and create a thick mesh with no transparent highlights. The brushwork is hard and clean. Even where it becomes entangled into inextricable knots of dry tendrils or nervous spirals, it always impresses by its simplicity. It gives the effect of a black silhouette, as concentrated and thick as a glutinous lump of cooling metal. Chillida's drawing displays something rather like a schema of the *opus metallicus* which transforms the shapeless mass and brings it to the point where art will seize on it and torture and mangle it so fiercely that it will bear its stamp for ever.

In these drawings Chillida seems to be straining to achieve something which comes naturally when he is working with hammer and tongs. When he is drawing he is concerned with the gossamer-thin layer of space whose depth is no more than suggested by the fine mesh which covers the paper and veins it with uneven fibres; it is an intricate system of twirls, curly arabesques, spiky trellises, nervous tendrils and blunted splinters. Sometimes the whole web works loose or pulls noisily apart; quick trills are interpolated and minute chinks appear, clawing out in all directions towards nothingness. His hand is no longer compelled to repeat the same gestures obstinately over and over again until the form submits; instead it follows the direction of the principle which guides it. The point of departure is fixed as abruptly as the final stroke. We seem to see a thread uncoiling itself as it winds through subterranean labyrinths, while an intricate network of arteries emerges from the deep to the light of day. The dualism which underlies this undulating or tangled handwriting is expressed in firm, curving lines and brushstrokes. The combination of the individual characters, the inter-connecting spaces between them and the void emanating from them does not create a single shape, but forms a series of eddies which reveal the dynamism of the brushwork.

We find the same linear force at work in the fantastic and austere geometry of his iron sculptures, and here too it links together tiny particles to form one continuous whole. The resistance offered by the material forces the form to undergo a slow and laborious, yet at the same time irresistible process of development. At certain points short segments are incorporated; they project from the basic structure, which acts as a sort of spinal column, and they are dependent on it, just as the network of tiny lines is in the drawings. Each spatial layer contradicts the orientation of the whole. Yet in spite of all these aberrations, the original axis runs right through the sculpture and indeed, it is this very discordance which gives it its driving force. The void is by now neither a spatial framework nor a spatial structure, but represents the invariable path of a movement; it is now an abstract image which follows a pre-arranged schema in drawing all possible inferences from a theme which is in itself indifferent—we might call it a plastic fugue.

Many of these sculptures result from the juxtaposition of elements which counteract one another until they reach a crescendo of tensions (pl. 18). These rectangular notes, arranged into chords and sequences, which clash and then are reconciled, transcribe the wild song of the forge. But there is the simple music, too, of a one-part song (pl. 20) This sculpture, which is always slipping away, branching off and changing direction, makes us think of tongs or levers prising up huge weights. Even the tiniest offshoot has the same undiminished power as the starting-point.

Every now and then the volume expands. It fills out and encroaches on the surrounding zone, filling it to overflowing (pls. 20-26) The roughness and fleshiness of the form softens the severity of its outline and blunts the aggressiveness of its contours. The form no longer wants to act as the line of demarcation which circumscribes the space. Instead of progressing by means of angular links, its energy now develops in bursts of controlled power which dart out from the iron stem rising from a vertical plinth; the volumes curve upwards from this plinth, just as white-hot metal does on the anvil.

Many of these *Anvils* look like lumps of metal squeezed tightly one inside the other and split by yawning crevices, with the space wedged into them (pl. 28). We also find slim ones which tower up and then plunge down, giving the effect of ships in an ethereal sea (pl. 34). Then the volume becomes enmeshed with the void once more; it surrounds it by tracing a rising spiral in the air and is itself enveloped by the circular movement; it seems to have hardened into a permanently rotating movement. The individual segments are grooved so that they can intersect and at the same time dissect the space. The anatomy of these explosive rhythms makes us think of the schematic statements of some cosmic mechanism or of the individual components of a primeval and half-broken machinery.

The form passes from the hollow shell, which is both extended and limited by the pauses and sudden turns of the spiral, to more cramped and involved modulations; these modulations are articulated by elements arranged in parallel or contrasting pairs and form an endless chain (pl. 32). The unconnected rhythms and the close similarity between convex and concave produce unsteady constellations and a dynamic instability. Currents of space are conducted through the framework created by the volumes. The limbs of this skeleton are arranged round the void and embrace it with their whole weight, compressing what little remains of the space, until they virtually efface it completely, suggesting it only by concealing it. In the earlier works a configuration, a tangible representation of space, resulted from the lines and volumes which gave it substance and from the contours which gave it life. Now that the space has been squeezed into the form, it portrays the form's unseen side, its negative image, and so must correspond exactly to the visible elements of which it is made up.

Thus the substance, revealed by a geometry which works in secret, is linked to the void which it includes with its surface. We are concerned, unlike in architecture, with real, not fictitious volume. An immaterial substance tallies with the material substance and is equally important to the whole system of forces and tensions. So this is the *raison d'être* of Chillida's work: to pursue space and track it down; to allow it to move freely and flexibly within the field of force to which it is subject; to let it circulate among the solid substances which contain it, concrete yet never present, real yet imaginary, determining yet determined. It does not, however, involve separating the form from some contradictory and hypothetical content for which it is supposed to provide a receptacle. The visible portion is there to represent its opposite; every form has its counter-form in which lies the basis of all its essential characteristics. Within the form the conflicting rhythms and tensions achieve harmony, contradictions support each other, and all values have different symptoms and become interchangeable.

The combinations of square volumes have since been developed by Chillida into a framework of heavy planks, in which their forces are calibrated and braced together. The wood keeps its natural grained surface and is rough and full of knot-holes. As with forged metal it shows the traces left by axe and hammer blows, the wounds to which it owes its form. Three of these pieces which transform the shapelessness crystallized round a core of emptiness illustrate different stages in Chillida's quest for the intangible. They correspond to the three main phases in the technique of metal sculpture: deployment on a horizontal plane (pl. 36), concentrated flight raised and supported by the void (pl. 37); and finally organized welding together and disciplined growth (pl. 39).

The solid mass of asymmetric blocks, soldered together by an irresistible power of attraction, rests quietly in it sponderous and imperturbable unity. All its different elements work together and all are ready to submit. The whole mass is framed by angles and edges. Yet chinks and gaps do force their way out somehow, without affecting its integrity. Gaps, geometric incisions and narrow slits steal into the depths and break off obliquely as if their course had been altered by some unknown force. Once inside they open out into unexpected hollows and run into inaccessible cavities and dead ends. Tiny "glimpses" occasionally indicate the existence of the void and suggest that there is a hidden presence lurking at the bend of each impasse.

At the very heart of the material, weighed down as it is by shapes and forms, the space foils all attempts to penetrate it; instead, it is the space which penetrates the material. This inner sanctuary of radiant emptiness which constitutes the hidden soul of the work can only be reached by a dark fissure. The negative form is immured in a shell formed by the volumes, and no longer vibrates in the midst of the tensions to which it is exposed. It is sealed among the haunts of a labyrinth which is filled with its noiseless language. The positive elements are illuminated from within by this darkness, by this prison which is both finite and infinite.

So, too, the spirit creates within itself the void from which its visions emanate. We might draw an analogy between the secret confines of the soul, which has renounced all external images, between what St John of the Cross calls the "mighty emptiness of the powers of the soul as its fullness overflows", and the withdrawal of the form in favour of the immanence which is its true goal.

There is a strange and undoubtedly deliberate relationship here between art and mysticism. The Taoists linked the impassible subterranean space within their "hollow mountain" to the "grotto-like chamber" which in their curious cerebral geography refers to the place where the mind, having dismissed the Self, enters the chaos of the world as yet uncreated. In the fourteenth century Suso described in similar terms the infinite depths of the chasm in which the whole of creation must perish. As with Tao's hollow vessel or the seething abysses of northern mythologies, we are concerned here with a sort of mystic crucible in which all individual phenomena are fused into an incandescent whole.

Sculpture, too, touches on these hidden secrets. If music sometimes has the power to describe the indescribable, sculpture is equally able (and sometimes even better able) to resolve the conflicts which arise between the form and that which is incompatible with it, between the concrete image and the numinous whose existence no art has yet succeeded in revealing without at the same time betraying it. The tiny fragment of space left is enough for the riddle to be posed and then solved in the sculptor's work. We are not privileged to see what is sacred. But the form identifies this sacred presence with space —which is in its turn the essence of form— and embodies it without betraying it. In his powerful and rigorous monstrances Chillida retains in full measure the two worlds of music and silence.

1

2

3   4

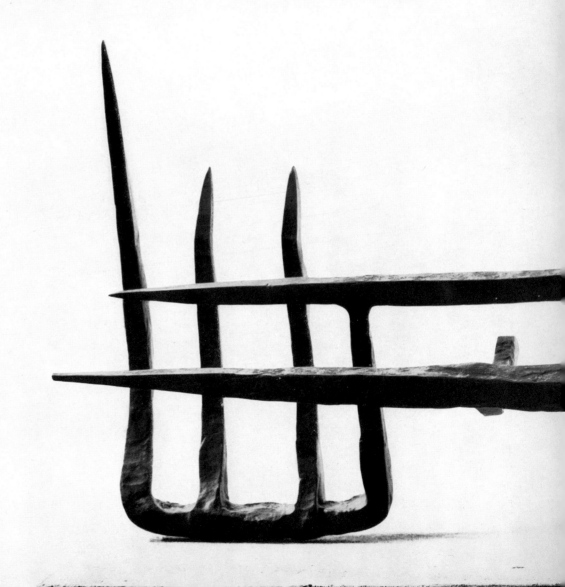

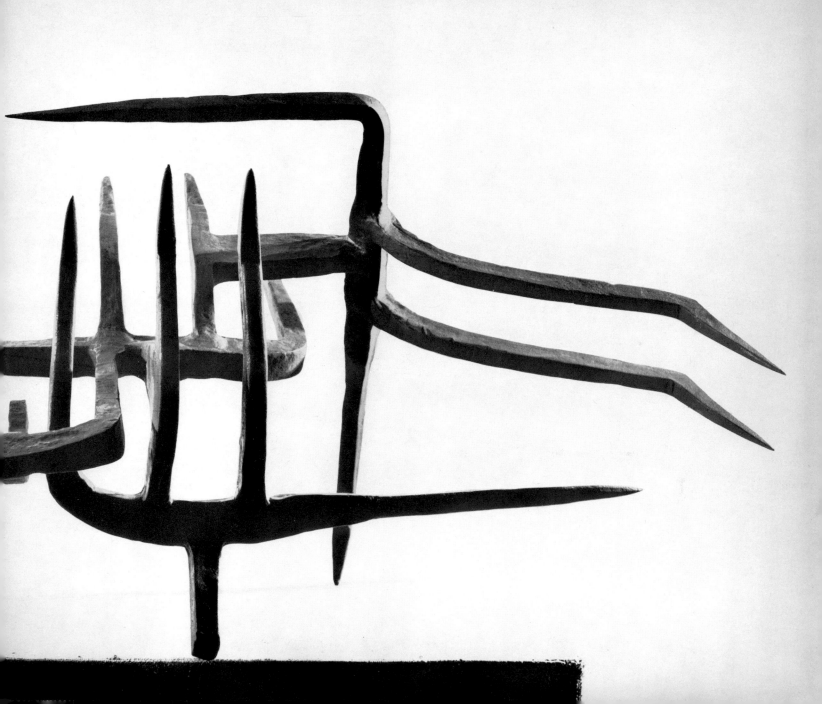

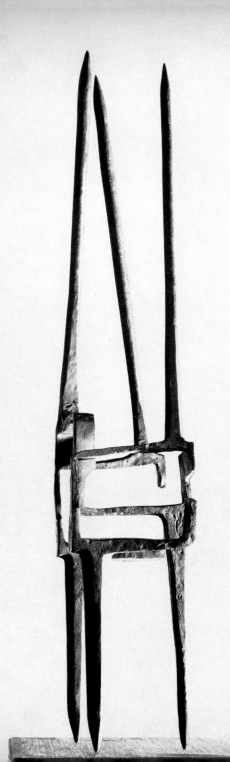

14

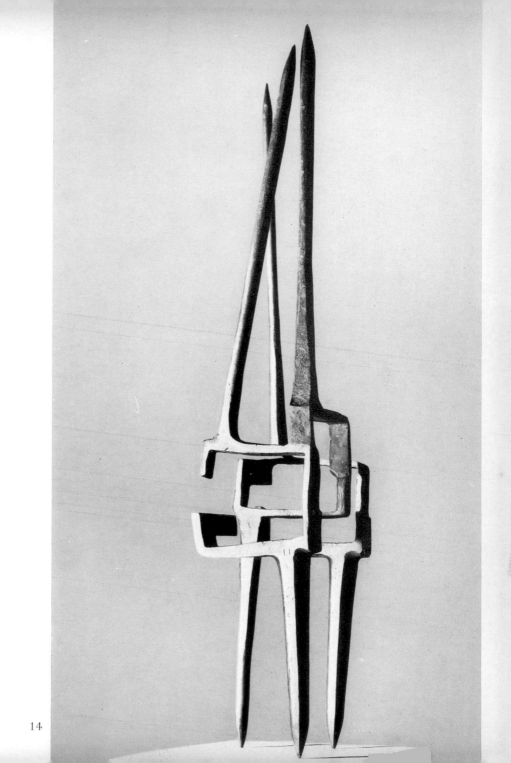

15

16

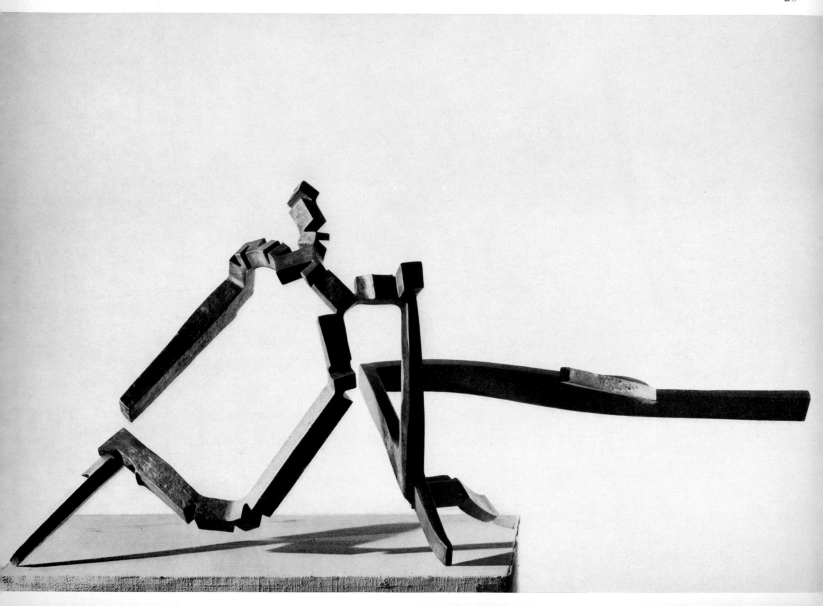

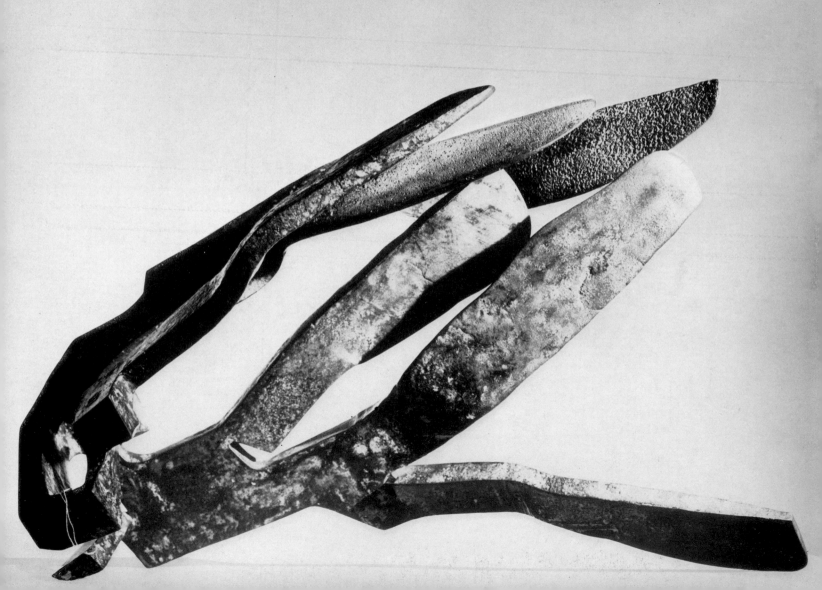

32

34

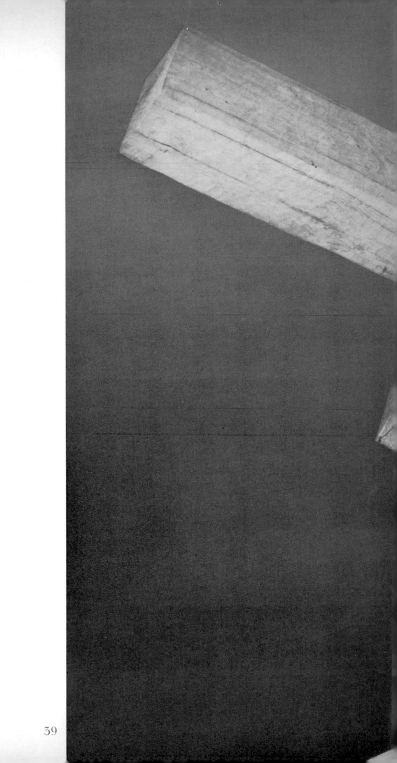

39

◁ 40, 41

1924	Eduardo Chillida born in San Sebastián, Spain, on 10 January. His music- and art-loving family lives in San Sebastián where Chillida spends his childhood. At school, he would sometimes play truant and set off alone on expeditions to the cliffs of Monte Egueldo on the coast.
1942	Studies architecture in Madrid. But Chillida has a different conception of architecture from that of the teaching programme. Art for him is an adventure that will open up new paths.
1945	Musical experience when he hears Schubert's *Rosamunde*.
1947	He gives up his architectural studies, and spends another year in Madrid where he registers at a private art school. He draws without a teacher and devotes himself with passionate interest to the analysis of form. He recognizes his vocation as a sculptor.
1949	He exhibits a torso in the *Salon de Mai* and executes others of which only one, a male torso, remains.
1950	He takes part in the group exhibition *Les Mains Eblouies* in the Galerie Maeght, Paris (October). He marries and settles in Villènes (Seine-et-Oise). He concentrates fully on his work. Transition to abstraction.
1951	Leaves Paris and moves to Hernani near San Sebastián. In the next four years he executes a large number of works which he does not exhibit (*Ilarik, From Within, Deseoso, Tres, Redondo al Rededor, Comb of Wind* etc).
1954	First one-man exhibition in the Clan Gallery, Madrid (April). Honorary diploma from the Milan Triennale. Four iron doors for the basilica of Aranzazu.
1955	Takes part in the exhibition *Eisenplastik* in the Kunsthalle, Bern; and in the *Premier Salon de la Sculpture Abstraite* in the Galerie Denise René, Paris. Monument for Sir Alexander Fleming in San Sebastián. First one-man exhibition in the Galerie Maeght, Paris (27 works, preface to the catalogue by Gaston Bachelard).
1957	He settles in San Sebastián. Takes part in the exhibition *Escultura al aire libre*, Madrid.

1958   Exhibition *Sculpture and Drawings from Seven Sculptors* in the Solomon
R. Guggenheim Museum, New York.
Exhibits in the XXIX Venice Biennale and gains the *Premio del Comune di
Venezia per la Scultura*.
Sculpture prize of the Graham Foundation, Chicago.
Takes part in the exhibition *Carnegie Institute International*, Pittsburgh.

1959   Takes part in numerous exhibitions: San Francisco Museum of Art; North
Carolina Museum of Art; Minneapolis Institute of Art; Los Angeles County
Museum; *Documenta II*, Kassel; *Blanco y Negro* (Darro Gallery, Madrid);
European Art To-day (Graham Foundation), etc.
First wood sculptures.

1960   Kandinsky prize.
Takes part in the exhibition *European Sculpture and Paintings* in the
B. Schaefer Gallery, New York; and the exhibition *De Daumier à nos jours*
in St Etienne.

1961   One-man exhibition in the Galerie Maeght, Paris (sculpture, drawings and
collages). Catalogue *Derrière le Miroir*, No. 124, with four original litho-
graphs, including two double-spreads; preface by J.J. Sweeney.
Takes part in the exhibition *The American Federation of Arts*, New York;
in the *Salon de la Jeune Sculpture* in the Musée Rodin, Paris; the exhibition
Three Spaniards, Picasso, Miró, Chillida in the Houston Museum, Texas;
in the *I Exposición de Arte Actual* in the Museo San Telmo, San
Sebastián.

1962   Takes part in the exhibition *Art since 1950*, Seattle; one-man exhibition in
the Kunsthalle, Basle (32 works, preface to the catalogue by Franz Meyer).
Takes part in the *Retrospective Exhibition of the Biennale Prizewinners*,
Venice; the exhibition *Some Directions in Modern Sculpture* in the Provi-
dence Arts Club, Rhode Island where he receives a prize; in the *Exposición
Venta pro-Damnificados del Valles*, Barcelona.

1963   Exhibition of drawings and collages in the Galerie Sankt Stephan, Vienna.

1964   Takes part in the exhibition *Cinquante Ans de Collages* in the Musée d'Art et d'Industrie, St Etienne, then in the Musée des Arts Décoratifs, Paris. Exhibition in the Kunsthaus, Zürich.

Exhibition of drawings in the Günther Franke Gallery, Munich.

Takes part in the exhibition *Carnegie Institute International*, Pittsburgh; in *Documenta III*, Kassel; in the exhibition *Painting and Sculpture of a Decade, '54–'64* in the Tate Gallery, London.

One-man exhibition in the Galerie Maeght, Paris (April) (10 works, including the wood sculptures *Abesti Gogora*, nos. 2 and 3). Catalogue *Derrière le Miroir*, No. 143, preface by Carola Giedion-Welcker.

Carnegie Prize in the 1964 *Pittsburgh International*.

Takes part in the exhibition *Collages by Painters and Sculptors*, with artists from five nations, in the B. Schaefer Gallery, New York.

Visits Greece.

1965   One-man exhibition in the McRoberts and Tunnard Gallery, London (preface to the catalogue by Roland Penrose).

1966   Receives North-Rhine prize, Westfalen, Dusseldorf. Awarded the Wilhelm Lehmbruck sculpture prize by the town of Duisburg, January.

One-man exhibition in Duisburg.

One-man exhibition in the Museum of Fine Arts in Houston, Texas. The granite sculpture, *Abesti Gogora*, no. 5, is commissioned for this Museum. Does illustrations for the book by A. Frénaud *Le Chemin des Devins*, published by Maeght, Paris.

1967   One-man exhibition at the Munson Williams Proctor Institute, Utica. City Art Museum, St. Louis.

Takes part in the exhibitions: *Dix ans d'Art vivant, 1955–65*, Fondation Maeght, St Paul; *Spanish Art of Today*, Nuremberg, Berlin, Baden-Baden; *Sculpture since 1965*, Chicago Art Institute; *Guggenheim International Exhibtion*, Solomon R. Guggenheim Museum, New York; *Carnegie International*, Pittsburgh.

Selected Bibliography

José de Castro Arines, 'Un escultor, Chillida', *Informaciones*, April 1954

Ettore Sottsass jr., 'Eduardo Chillida, escultor', *Domus*, no. 306, May 1955

J. A., 'Chillida', *Cimaise*, November/December 1956

L. D., 'Chillida', *Aujourd'hui*, November 1956

Gaston Bachelard, 'Le cosmos du fer', *Derrière le Miroir*, no. 90–91, Oct./Nov. 1956

Juan Antonio Gaya Nuño, 'Chillida, escultor en hierro caliente', *Insula*, 15.2.1957

Juan Mayor, 'Los hierros de Chillida', *Indice*, Madrid, May 1957

Ricardo Gullon, 'Chillida', *Cuadernos Hispano-Americanos* no. 85, 1957

J. J. Tharrats, *Artistas de hoy*, 'Eduardo Chillida', Barcelona n. d.

Pierre Volboudt, 'Chillida', *XXe Siecle*, no. 8, Paris 1957

Juan Eduardo Cirlot, 'La escultura de Eduardo Chillida', *Papeles de Son Armadans*, no. XLIII, October 1959

Vicente Aguilera Cerni, 'La nuova scultura spagnola', Venice Biennale, July–Sept. 1960

J. J. Sweeney, 'Eduardo Chillida', *Derrière le Miroir*, no. 124, March 1961

M. F. Prieto Barral, 'Los hierros de Chillida en Paris', *España*, 2–8 May 1961

S. M. 'Eduardo Chillida', Venice Biennale, March 1961

John Ashberry, 'Chillida and others', *Art International*, 1 May 1961

Carola Giedion-Welcker, *Contemporary Sculpture. An Evolution in Volume and Space.* London, 1961

Franz Meyer, 'Eduardo Chillida', Catalogue preface. Kunsthalle, Basle, 3 March 1962

A Dictionary of Modern Sculpture (ed. Maillard), London, 1962

Maria Netter, 'Der baskische Bildhauer Eduardo Chillida', *Werk*, 6 January 1962

M. P. F., 'Sensación en Paris ante una exposición de Chillida', *ABC*, Madrid, 1962

Torres Murillo, 'Eduardo Chillida', *Revista Obras*, no. 98, 1962

P. Restany, 'Un janséniste basque, Chillida', *Cimaise*, no. 60, July–August 1962

Umbro Apollonio, 'Eduardo Chillida', *Siderexport*, no. 4, 1962

Carola Giedion-Welcker, 'La poésie de l'espace chez E. Chillida', *Derrière le Miroir*, no. 143, April 1964

Pierre Volboudt, 'Espace sacré, espace profane', *XXe Siècle*, no. XXIV, 1964

Miguel Perez Ferrero, 'Chillida o el Espíritu de los Bascos', *ABC*, Madrid, 10 May 1964

'*Chillida*', España Semanal, 14 July 1964

Roland Penrose, 'Chillida'. Catalogue preface. McRoberts and Tunnard Gallery, London, May 1965

Charles S. Spencer, 'Chillida', *Studio International*, June 1965

Gerhard Händler, 'Eduardo Chillida'. Catalogue preface. Wilhelm Lehmbruck Museum, Duisburg, 7 May 1966

J. J. Sweeney, 'Eduardo Chillida'. Catalogue preface. The Museum of Fine Arts, Houston, Texas, 4 October 1966

E. W., 'Eduardo Chillida'. Catalogue preface. Buchholz Gallery, Munich, October–November 1966

Carola Giedion-Welcker, 'Chillida', *Quadrum*, no. 20, 1966

José Maria Moreno-Galvan, 'Chillida', *Triunfo*, 29 April 1967

Werner Schmalenbach, 'Chillida'. Catalogue preface. Alex Vömel Gallery, Dusseldorf, March-April 1967

List of Photographers

All photographs were taken by the artist with the exception of the following:
Brenwasser, New York: 3; Budd, New York: 40; Franco Cianetti, Paris: 10, 13, 14, 15, 16, 17, 18, 19, 20, 22, 26, 29, 31, 37; Gallerie Maeght, Paris: 1, 2, 5, 12, 23, 27, 34, 35, 38, 39, 41; O. E. Nelson, New York: 9; Öffentliche Kunstsammlung, Basle: 33; The Museum of Fine Arts, Houston: 36; The Solomon R. Guggenheim Museum, New York: 8.